Huddle Up

Huddle Up

CREATING AND SUSTAINING A
CULTURE OF SERVICE EXCELLENCE

ROBERT L. COOPER

Copyright © 2004 by Robert L. Cooper.
ISBN: Softcover   1-4134-4558-6

All rights reserved. No part of this book may be reproduced or transmitted in any form or by any means, electronic or mechanical, including photocopying, recording, or by any information storage and retrieval system, without permission in writing from the copyright owner.

The Organizational Huddle Process is a trademark of Robert L. Cooper, all rights reserved worldwide. Rated as a Grade A Best Practice by the Advisory Board Company.

This book was printed in the United States of America.

To order additional copies of this book, contact:
Xlibris Corporation
1-888-795-4274
www.Xlibris.com
Orders@Xlibris.com

Contents

INTRODUCTION 7

CHAPTER I: GET YOUR TEAM ON THE FIELD 11

CHAPTER II: WE WIN TOGETHER 14

CHAPTER III: RUN WITH THE BALL 18

CHAPTER IV: FUMBLES WILL HAPPEN 22

CHAPTER V: WE ARE ALL LEADERS 24

CHAPTER VI: IT'S ALL ABOUT RELATIONSHIPS 27

CHAPTER VII: FRONT OFFICE SUPPORT 29

CHAPTER VIII: THE HUDDLE IN ACTION 31

FINAL THOUGHTS 41

FREQUENTLY ASKED QUESTIONS 43

TESTIMONIALS 47

Introduction

This Leader's Guide is written with great passion and enthusiasm. For over twenty years as a practitioner in the fields of human resources and organizational development, I have searched for strategies and methodologies to improve individual and group performance. The Organizational Huddle Process™ came to me as I watched the New York Jets during a preseason game in the summer of 1999. I visualized business professionals on the playing field looking face to face with a common goal – to win together. On the surface, the solution seems obvious and fairly easy. If we bring individuals together on a regular basis to collaborate and support each other in "running the next play," we all win. As a practitioner, I believed that the challenge was to create a process that is relatively easy to implement, enjoyable for participants, and yet quite complex relative to the dynamics that will make it effective. The Organizational Huddle™ transforms complexity into a very usable and extremely effective way to conduct business. The concept is based on the New Sciences, a fresh new way to create high-performance organizations. The New Sciences focuses on quantum physics as opposed to Newtonian science – the science of certainty and predictability. Newtonian organizations maintain control from the top and are highly inflexible. Quantum organizations look at the connections throughout the hierarchy, and not just the isolated parts. This enables individuals throughout the organization to see each other as customers and effectively manage complexity, chaos, and uncertainty. The Organizational Huddle™ provides the tool that enables individuals at all levels to meet today's challenges.

The analogy to football is very interesting. When we observe a football game, things seem fairly clear. Each team attempts to move the ball and score points more than the other team. What we do not see are the variables that create and sustain success. We are not exposed to the planning sessions teams conduct, the relationships between players (other than what we may read in the newspaper or watch on television), or the commitment of the coaches and players. Similarly, the Organizational Huddle Process™ has the inherent challenge of bringing individuals with different beliefs, preferences, styles, motivations, and commitment altogether to drive positive results for each other and the customers they serve. The power of the Organizational Huddle™ is that it is ongoing and provides the opportunity for groups to develop trust and cohesiveness through direct, fast, and timely communications. It empowers individuals to resolve problems with speed, focus, and confidence. The challenge is managing the human factor. Transforming individuals and groups from silos to partners, from indirect communicators to direct ones, from finger pointers to supporters into fully accountable professionals is absolutely possible. The Organizational Huddle Process™ is an excellent complement to Total Quality Management and Business Redesign. This methodology will very often resolve problems quickly without the need for the lengthy analysis found in other processes. When an issue cannot be handled through the Huddle, then a decision may be made to forward through a Performance Improvement Process. Any leader focused on developing a service-excellence culture can benefit greatly by implementing this concept.

For those inspiring leaders out there, this guide is for you. I want to directly connect with you because you understand that people, not machines or technology, produce business results.

Our goal is to ignite our employees and allow them to express their abilities, creativity, and desires. I truly believe that building strong relationships enables business groups to thrive. Let us build those relationships and enhance performance. Our employees and customers deserve our best efforts. This has already proven to be a breakthrough that develops excellent teams, resolves and prevents problems, significantly enhances customer satisfaction, and impacts organizational effectiveness. Thus far, over one thousand issues have been expediently resolved at organizations utilizing this methodology, with a tremendous increase in stakeholder satisfaction.

This guide should initially be read cover to cover and then used as a reference as needed. Each chapter provides insight into both the process and the underlying principles that drive its success. At the end of each chapter, a summary of the key learning points is provided. A few examples of organizations that have successfully implemented this process are included in the section "Huddle in Action." I wish you the best of luck as you step onto the playing field, and may your organization always win the Superbowl.

Robert L. Cooper

Chapter 1

Get Your Team on the Field

Have you ever thought about why many teambuilding programs fail to sustain long-term positive gains? It is true that many employees leave a teambuilding session all juiced up and rearing to go, but then things seem to fizzle. You ask why – after all you spent $2,000 on a top-notch consultant. Or you purchased the latest off-the-shelf program guaranteed to bring you excellent results in thirty days or less or your money back. The answer lies in the fact that, just like the best football teams, you cannot win without everyone touching or seeing the ball, or at least showing up on the playing field. In the 1969 Superbowl, most experts said the New York Jets had absolutely no chance to beat the mighty Baltimore Colts. I remember being at my cousin's wedding listening to one of her many friends say the game will be over by halftime. I was upset that I was missing this great event; how can a wedding be scheduled on Superbowl Sunday? I wondered if Joe Namath knew something the experts did not when he guaranteed that the New York Jets would win. The Jets won the game and proved the point that if a team pulls together and believes in itself, anything is possible. In the business world, many of us go through our day-to-day activities as if we are sitting on the bench not participating. We do not think it is important to know what our teammates are thinking or who needs to run with the ball. We believe that our means of communication is effective. After all you sent Joe the E-mail, he should know what you want, when you want it, and how you want it. When the report comes to you with 25 percent of what you requested had been omitted, you ask your secretary to get Joe on the phone. You then discover that Joe will be out of town for the next ten days. You ask your secretary to track Joe down. He finally calls you back three days later and says, "That's not what you asked me to do." You insist that you must get the revised document by tomorrow. Joe explains that he is very busy and cannot attend to this matter until next Monday. It is clear that you and Joe are not singing from the same playbook.

Why is it that some quarterbacks and wide receivers have such great success? I have marveled at the incredible connection between Joe Montana and Jerry Rice when they played together on the San Francisco 49ers. Montana had such grace as a quarterback, and Rice is probably the greatest wide receiver to ever play the game of football. I do not believe it was their individual greatness alone that made them gel. They had a very special bond – an incredible awareness to each other's needs. Montana knew where Rice was, and Rice knew where Montana was at all times. They could never enjoy the moments together in the spotlight of Superbowl Sunday without getting onto the playing field.

The playing field is a place where individuals look at each other, listen to each other's needs, and enjoy meeting those needs. The playing field is not always magical or as exciting as the roar of the crowd on a beautiful autumn Sunday afternoon in a professional football stadium. The playing field is a real place in the life of all business professionals. It is where championships are won and lost. It is an opportunity to move our organization toward a Superbowl championship. It is a place where we can all be Joe Montana or Jerry Rice. It is where we can share our visions, our needs, and our support for each other. The world of business requires connections, compassion, and spirit. Have you ever asked the fundamental question why some quarterbacks with outstanding talent fail, and others with average talent thrive? The winners know that they are only as successful as the team around them. Have you ever wondered why some business professionals with outstanding credentials fail while others with average credentials are so successful? Do you want to enjoy the success of Joe Montana and Jerry Rice? If you do, then it is time for you to get onto the playing field . . . let's huddle up.

Lesson I Learning Points

- Create an informal space for participants to collaborate. A section of a cafeteria or special huddle room without tables is ideal.
- Identify individuals who have natural customer relationships and rely on each other daily for support.
- Huddles can be inter-departmental or intra-departmental with several departments or job classifications represented.
- All participants are involved and support each other to ensure optimum customer satisfaction.
- The Huddle is fast, lasting no more than ten to fifteen minutes on average (never exceed thirty minutes).
- It is imperative that each participating department or job classification attends the huddle on time or sends a representative. Rotation of membership is strongly recommended.
- The Huddle is a two-dimensional process that resolves and prevents problems while building strong business relationships.

Chapter II

We Win Together

As I think back to my first memories of football, I see the image of Vince Lombardi, the great coach of the Greenbay Packers, walking up and down the sidelines on a cold Sunday afternoon. I wish I could have had the opportunity to sit down with Mr. Lombardi and talk about the concepts of team, focus, accountability, and vision. What did he see as the quarterback's role in winning, the running back, offensive linemen, etc?

The thing that resonates with me is the idea that winning, regardless of our definition, means that everyone on the team wins. If we do not win, it was a team effort, no room to blame anyone. In many of my workshops, I have participants explore an even deeper meaning of team – the concept of ensemble. The definition of an ensemble is a unit or group of complementary parts contributing to a single effect. It is the outcome that matters, placing emphasis on results and not individual contributions. This does not mean that you relinquish individuality or do not acknowledge individual contributions along the way. The focus is placed on group results toward a common goal.

I have attained an appreciation to the music group Nsync. Watch the movements on stage, the interdependence of each artist, the blending of the music, the ability to move out of the spotlight. Football, like music, recognizes each individual's talent, but more importantly understands that winning is everything. And when the team wins, we all win. In football, winning the game satisfies the team's loyal fans. In music, winning the support of followers and the acknowledgment of critics is the goal. In organizations, we must strive to define winning as giving our internal and external customers what they need, and if possible, exceed those expectations.

The Organizational Huddle Process™ has a fundamental respect for each participant's skills and abilities. The primary focus is placed on supporting each other to provide the best service to our customers. That is the true definition of winning in an organizational context. The question we must ponder is, if winning is satisfying our customers, who are our customers? Why do we sometimes fall short of winning the game?

Let's start with the first question: who are our customers? We have many customers, other departments, our staff, our community, and the individuals consuming our products and services. We often fail to meet our customer's needs due to broken processes or too many egos at the table. When Bill Walsh took over as coach of the San Francisco 49ers, he was given credit for implementing the West Coast offense. This highly sophisticated system was recognized as being a key ingredient in the success of the 49ers and put Joe Montana on the map. Initiating new processes is important; recognizing that winning as an ensemble is of greater significance. What if Joe Montana thought that he was the center of the universe, perhaps he would try to do too much himself. In business, the out-of-control ego is one of the greatest obstacles that keep us from winning. This is played out on the business field in often subtle ways, and often not so subtle. This is the individual who believes that nothing positive can or will happen without their involvement. This is the individual who, during a meeting, will not listen to other points of view. In sports, we see quite often a player being traded because of their inability to buy into the team concept. Paradoxically, we reward individualism and often condemn that same individualism when team chemistry is affected. One fact is absolutely true: In both sports and business, no individual is greater than the contributions of the whole. How is that possible? These players are paid tremendous amounts of money. This proves that although individual contributions need to be respected, winning as a team is the only thing. In business, we often pay enormous salaries to individuals and give them plush carpeting and the corner office. We delude ourselves into thinking that these individuals unilaterally determine success. I am not suggesting that their visions are not critical; however, it is the individuals closest to the customer who truly defines winning. Who is really on the playing field day in and day out, in the trenches making things happen? Our challenge continues to be how to unleash these individuals' talents and get out of their way. Yes, we could do wonderful things for our customers in an environment of support, fun, and informality. A setting where the landscape is flattened, where individual talent blends with others to make a beautiful mosaic. A place where customer needs are resolved and laughter can be found. It may be a beautiful Monday morning without the need to play Monday morning quarterback. No need for second-guessing, just a focus on getting it right. Just a place to say, "How was your weekend and how can I help you?" The opportunity to say "thanks for your support" and "have a great day." True collaboration enables us to win without feeling pain. I recommend you put this book down right now if you prefer to sweat it out. If you choose to send many E-mails, set up several long meetings that are time wasters, cover your tail, and continue to play the corporate political game. I urge you to read no further. The time has come that we realize that we always win when we collaborate effectively. You cannot win the Superbowl without it. Are you ready to take the handoff and carry the ball?

Lesson 2 Learning Points

- The Organizational Huddle™ fosters the concept of ensemble; we are all important and contribute to group success.

- Everyone is an equal participant, regardless of title.
- Success is defined as providing internal and external customers with the support required to meet identified needs.
- Mutual respect is a value inherent in the Huddle process.
- Collaboration is not only a value spoken; it becomes part of the fabric of the organization.

Chapter III

Run with the Ball

Walter Peyton, the former Chicago Bear running back, was a man who played with heart and passion – a true champion. He always seemed to want the ball, especially in key situations. Why is it that some people desire to carry the ball, and others do not? You cannot score without the ball. Teams cannot be successful if participants are reluctant to touch the ball. I am not talking about taking the ball with the expectation to glow in the spotlight. I refer to the desire to hold the ball with the goal of attaining a positive gain. It's about heart, focus, purpose, and passion. Failure to step up to the plate and give it your best shot is not acceptable, if you want to be considered a contributor. When the ball is placed in your hand, move with confidence and conviction. Sure, you may get hit; then again you may even score. Either way, it does not matter. You owe it to yourself and teammates to move and give it your best shot. In business, do you run with the ball or turn your back on situations? Are you afraid of being accountable to your team? You may ask, "What if I do not deliver?" The bigger question is, "What if you do not try?" The Organizational Huddle Process™ is played on a field where balls are constantly handed off. Someone may say,

"Sally, I need you to send me a revised procedure by Thursday." The expectation is that Sally will run with the ball and deliver. Sally needs to see other members of the huddle as internal customers, people depending on her commitment to serve. If Sally cannot meet the request, she must negotiate and attain agreement on the time frame. Reaching the end zone a day late without having a meeting of the minds with your customer is not acceptable. It is a breach of integrity! When this occurs, the Monday morning quarterbacks come out in force to question Sally's movements. They say things like "Had Sally done this or that then maybe she would have delivered the goods." The name of the game is for the organization to win. This requires clean handoffs from one person to another, with the willingness to accept the challenge. If Sally's focus is on her needs only, then perhaps she will settle for a three-yard gain. It has always amazed me how many people approach their jobs with the mindset that their needs are greater than their teammates. Running with the ball means stepping into accountability. Yes, you are expected to move toward the goal line. Fumbles will happen, but winners get up and go after the ball with tenacity. If fear is your enemy, then you will never ask for or accept the ball. The dilemma faced is that unless you live in isolation on a deserted island, the ball will always be coming your way. The issue is not "Will you accept the ball?" but rather "Will you step into responsibility and move?" Failure to accept the ball could mean that you will be cut from the team. Unlike football, in business you can always ask for help in the middle of a play. You may need to hand the ball off to an assistant. The Organizational Huddle Process™ requires all individuals to accept the ball and see to it that results are delivered. Participants determine how to get the job done. When you hand the ball off to your assistant, it is still your ball. The accountability does not stop because someone else is handling the ball. The huddle expects that you get the job done. This requires that the person to whom you handed the ball off to see you as their customer. When the starting quarterback leaves the game, the back-up quarterback has the ball. The final outcome is a reflection of both individuals' work.

We learn to recognize that all of our efforts are interconnected. Accountability should be embraced as another opportunity to contribute. It is through this desire to carry the ball that we learn and grow. How often do we hear about the reserve player not being prepared for game situations because they are standing on the sideline? The playing field is an opportunity to develop your skills and test your inner strength. It is a place where you take a few hits and benefit from it. If you run hard, keep the goal in mind, and focus, you usually score. Scoring leads to satisfied customers; they are provided with what they need. In football, it's scoring points. In business, it is resolving a problem, supplying information, or providing a service.

The Organizational Huddle™ is a game of trust. It is not a place of perfection. Mistakes can and will happen. Perhaps we did not communicate effectively and there was a misunderstanding of the need. I must let you know that my need was not met and you must respond. We must show respect for each other, recognizing that our working relationship is important for future success. The next time you will be expected to hold onto the ball tightly, move through the line, and reach the end zone. We must learn to have high expectations and be patient at the same time. We must learn not to point fingers or blame. We must learn that stepping into accountability allows for good things to happen. It is all about giving a solid effort when the ball is in your hands. Your teammates and customers depend on you, and as winners, we will not let them down.

Lesson 3 Learning Points

- All huddle participants must accept and follow-through on agreed-upon commitments.
- Each participant must step into accountability and communicate back to the huddle any unfulfilled agreements, and how the issue will be addressed.
- When a commitment is broken, participants need to show respect for the individual or department responsible.

Communicate what need is still unmet and allow for an explanation.
- Periodically ask, "Do we have any outstanding issues?" This ensures all previously communicated issues have been addressed.

Chapter IV

Fumbles Will Happen

One of the greatest fears a football player lives with is the possibility of the fumble. This becomes heightened when the game is on the line. Imagine that one minute is left on the game clock, your team is trailing by six points and the ball is on your opponent's five-yard line. The ball is placed in your hand; the defense is trying to knock the ball loose. You drop the ball, and the referee signals that the other team has recovered it. This is an athlete's worst nightmare playing out. How do you face your teammates? What can you say?

The ability to move beyond this unfortunate chain of events and come back stronger is the sign of a mature athlete. In business, fumbles will happen. Hopefully, they are not of the magnitude that will cost your team the game. The way in which we handle our fumbles are at the core of our personal integrity. Integrity does not mean perfection; it implies being true to yourself and others. When you fumble, do you blame someone else? Does the running back see the fumbles as being the offensive lineman's fault? After all, had he blocked the oncoming linebacker who knocked the ball away, this would not or could not have happened. We must all step into responsibility and not blame others for our fumbles. Many, many balls are handed off throughout the Huddle process. When you are asked to follow through on another department's concern, it is not acceptable to blame others for not getting the job done. You are accountable for all fumbles and asking for the ball again. Your teammates need to show respect for you even when a fumble occurs. It is through this process of mutual support that the group's cohesiveness develops. Others will want to see that you are making every effort to correct the problem. If you made a mistake, simply say, "I made a mistake; here is how I plan to resolve the issue." If you act as though the fumble is not your problem, your integrity is on the line. How could the huddle come to trust and rely on you? This is especially difficult since all participants saw the ball placed in your hands. The Organizational Huddle Process™ keeps all communication out in the open. Once you acknowledge that you will handle the problem given to you, the ball is all yours. Trust is built when you are seen as someone who can be counted on to get things done. The team will breakdown when individuals point fingers at each other, don't communicate openly, and fail to step into and maintain accountability. Remember, when you are handed the ball, follow-through, meet or exceed your customer's expectations, apologize for fumbles and never compromise your personal integrity.

Lesson 4 Learning Points

- When a customer need is not met, it is important for the responsible individual to resolve the issue. The participant that brought the issue to the huddle must show respect by raising the concern again and allowing for a satisfactory resolution.
- If issues are continuously not resolved, the integrity of the huddle would be compromised. The responsible individual would need to be counseled.

Chapter V

We Are All Leaders

Every football team has a quarterback, the individual who hands the ball off to a running back or throws to a wide receiver. The quarterback is expected to move the team toward the end zone and score points. When a team wins, the quarterback often gets much of the credit. When a team loses, the quarterback will assume a great deal of the blame. The quarterback calls the signals that let the team know what play is about to be run. In traditionally run organizations, the quarterback is usually the supervisor or manager. The staff is told what to do, how to do it, and are expected to complete the task efficiently. In most modern-day organizations, the staff is expected to know what to do, set their own direction, and monitor results. In a sense, the hierarchical pyramid is turned sideways, with everyone playing the quarterback role.

The Organizational Huddle™ requires each participant to see themselves as quarterbacks. We all have the opportunity to start the process and call the plays. This role assures that everyone has the opportunity to look for support or provide updates. Everyone has an equal voice at the huddle. It is not the title someone has that commands respect; it is the quality of their contribution. The playing field is a place where the customers' needs are placed in the middle of the table. We all contribute to the success of the process. If I play quarterback today, you may play quarterback the next time. The bottom line is it really doesn't matter; we all get to touch the ball.

Unfortunately, in business, not everyone gets to handle the ball. Many organizations talk about how they have empowered their workforce. The truth is many people do not feel as though they have the power. They believe they do not have the ability to set direction, offer new ideas or challenge past practices. The best ideas usually come from the people doing the job every day. All we have to do is ask them for their suggestions, give them freedom to act, and get out of the way. This requires senior leaders to view every staff member as a teammate, not a subordinate. Once we step onto the playing field, we are on equal footing. Sure, we know who the coach is, the general manager, and the best player. When it comes to deciding on the movement of the ball, the only thing that matters is who has the best idea at that moment. Strong egos and titles must be left at the door. The playing field has no room or tolerance for bureaucratic thinking.

Lesson 5 Learning Points

- All participants are given the opportunity to play the leader role.
- The huddle leader starts the process by going in rotation, asking participants if they have any issues requiring assistance from other members of the huddle. They also are requested to share updates on information that may benefit the other members of the huddle.
- The leader makes sure everyone understands the issue raised and that a commitment to resolve the concern is made. If the problem cannot be resolved within two minutes, the leader will suggest that the stakeholders involved meet outside of the huddle and bring their resolution back to the huddle. An

issue may be so complex that it needs to be forwarded to the Performance Improvement Process.
- The leader should take note of individuals or departments that did not attend the huddle. This may be forwarded to a "champion," an individual within the organization selected to oversee the Huddle process and ensure the integrity of the process.
- The leader will make note of accomplishments and forward to the "champion."

Chapter VI

It's All About Relationships

    We often hear football analysts talk about team chemistry. This is a feeling state, a sense of connection between people. You know that your teammates will do everything possible to assist you. This may be the offensive lineman blocking for the running back. Superbowls are not won solely on team chemistry. Each player's ability to execute according to the plan is critical. However, without strong relationships, it becomes increasingly more difficult to win the big game. If a quarterback believes that a wide receiver is not giving his all, the ball probably will not be thrown in that direction. Positive relationships are the driving force that sustains team spirit. Talking about building relationships in business is often seen as soft, with little to no parallel to results. Think about a coworker that you do not trust to support you. If a project is dependent on both of you collaborating and the relationship is less than positive, what will the outcome be? When the pressure builds, will you support each other? We often approach the business playing field as if it is time to put on our game face and the human side of the equation is not important. We fail to recognize that executing strategy has a foundation based on solid relationships.

The Organizational Huddle™ is a two-dimensional process. Dimension 1 involves the resolution of and prevention of problems. Dimension 2 is the building of relationships. This occurs as a result of mutual respect, delivering on promises, and learning to enjoy the collaborative process. It is through the building of relationships that will enable the group to achieve outstanding results. This happens naturally, as a by-product of the development of the human connection. This is where I support you and you support me. I trust you and you trust me. I respect you and you respect me. I enjoy working with you and you enjoy working with me. We learn to recognize that the only thing that matters is satisfying all of our customers. The beauty of this process is that when we are called upon to resolve even more difficult issues, the relationship is a driving force that makes it all possible. Politics does not enter into the equation. Our egos are checked at the door. It is plain and simple: You and I could focus on the problem and deliver the result. We are fully engaged in the world of win/win, mutual support to drive customer satisfaction allows us all to win the big game.

Lesson 6 Learning Points

- Building positive business relationships is a critical foundation for both the huddle and organizational success.
- Meeting each participant's needs is the key to the success of the huddle.
- Acknowledging other's support builds a sense of cohesiveness.

Chapter VII

Front Office Support

Nothing is more exciting for a football player than to play in the Superbowl. This is the culmination of dedication and hard work. This is center stage with the world watching. The team that executes the best, stays focused, makes the fewest mistakes, and adjusts effectively will win the game. What is not visible to most fans is the support of the team's executives, often referred to as the front office. The owners, president, general manager, and all support staff are all part of the equation. They are responsible for providing the best possible players and supporting the coach and the entire team throughout the season. Although they do not usually step onto the playing field, the fact that they show consistent support for the team is positive.

The Organizational Huddle™ requires senior management to be active supporters. This support is shown by assisting in selecting the initial huddles, promote the Huddle concept in various communication forums, periodically attend a huddle as a participant, and recognize individuals for their efforts. It is recommended that individuals in the organization be selected to champion the process. The individuals chosen should have excellent interpersonal skills and good facilitation abilities. They should work well with all levels in the organization and, most importantly, share the passion and commitment toward the Huddle process. These individuals will have the full support of senior leadership and are responsible for organizing the initial huddle(s) and ensuring the process gets off to a good start. They will need to be active catalysts in promoting the concept and maintain the integrity of the process. This means that individuals are attending the huddle on time, issues are resolved to complete customer satisfaction, and accomplishments are being recorded. Initially, these individuals should play the role of leader, and within a few sessions, relinquish the role and encourage a shared leadership model. It is recommended that after the initial huddle(s) are working well, expansion is to occur naturally, with those departments or individuals most interested to approach the champions. The beauty of this process is that it makes it easy to administer. No minutes, flipcharts, scheduling of meeting rooms (cafeteria is best or assign a special huddle room) are required. The informality and ease of execution is what participants have come to appreciate. "This does not feel like a meeting" is the very common statement participants make. Over time, the champion role becomes much easier as the process takes hold in the organization. Remember, although the process is fairly easy to implement, the complexity of the dynamics that make this methodology work are profound. This is a fundamental positive change process that deals with the most complex issue, the human equation.

Lesson 7 Learning Points

- Senior leadership plays a vital role in the Huddle process. They select and support champions, individuals with the responsibility to effectively implement the Huddle and monitor results.
- Senior leadership needs to promote the Huddle concept within the organization and periodically attend the huddle as a participant.
- The champions will play the leader role, during the implementation phase of the Huddle, and mentor others to assume the role in a shared leadership model.

Chapter VIII

The Huddle in Action

Organization 1 – Manufacturer of Industrial Components in New Jersey

This manufacturing company initiated the Huddle to address the following concerns:

- Poor and ineffective inter-departmental communication
- Lack of action and accountability to resolve issues
- Inability to identify current issues as they relate to overall organizational strategy and top management expectations
- Unclear understanding of each department's goals and objectives

The following huddles were established:

- Accounting, Purchasing, and Warehouse
- Purchasing, Marketing, and Inventory
- Marketing, Sales, and Information Technology

Outcomes:

To date, over one hundred problems have been quickly resolved. The following are a few examples:

- Development of a new procurement process
- Increased inventory turns
- Less obsolete or excess stock
- New policies for purchasing inventory
- Reduced stock-out positions
- Development of a web-based system for customers, leading to increased customer satisfaction
- Facilitated quotation and order acquisition process

Other Benefits Include:

- Fast problem identification and resolution
- High accountability to take action to resolve issues
- Significant increase in communication and teamwork

Organization 2 – Regional Medical Center in New Jersey

A regional medical center in New Jersey initiated the Organizational Huddle Process™ in the fall of 1999. The identified needs were to drive down decision making to the individuals or groups closest to the customer, develop collaborative relationships across organizational units, speed up decision making to resolve and prevent customer related issues, and enhance internal and external customer satisfaction. The following steps were taken to effectively implement and sustain success:

Step I: A meeting was held with members of senior management to discuss the Organizational Huddle™, expected outcomes, and implementation plan. The decision was made to develop an interdisciplinary huddle comprised of nurse managers and key internal suppliers. The nurse managers represent both unit staff and patient needs. The internal suppliers identified were those departments nursing most relies upon for support on a daily basis. The departments initially identified were Environmental Services, Maintenance, Security, Respiratory Therapy, Central Supply, Pharmacy, and Food and Nutrition. As the process evolved, several other functions joined the huddle.

Step II: A meeting was conducted with those individuals representing the departments participating in the huddle. The Nursing Division has over twenty managers; thus a decision to rotate representation (approximately two to three at a huddle) was made. Participants were trained on the Organizational Huddle Process™, roles and responsibilities, and keys to success.

Step III: The first "live" huddle was conducted in the employee cafeteria. This process is most effective when held in an informal setting. The employee cafeteria is conducive to a relaxed atmosphere and allows participants to collaborate while enjoying a cup of coffee or breakfast. The decision was to meet every Monday, Wednesday, and Friday at 8:30 AM. The expectation was made clear that all departments participating must be represented. The nurse managers attending represents all Nursing units. The process initiated in Nursing is that any unit that has an issue for the huddle needs to communicate their concerns to one of the nurse managers attending the huddle. The nurse managers in attendance communicate back to their colleagues on any issues that were brought up at the huddle that will impact them. The nurse managers are asked, "Any issues in Nursing?" These are communicated with the expectation that an internal supplier will resolve the need or an explanation of why this issue cannot be resolved will be given. I initially played the role of champion and leader. The leader's responsibility is to start the Huddle process, ensure all participants have the opportunity to share concerns or promote updates, and keep the process moving. After a few huddles, I relinquished the leader role to the director of safety and security. As the process evolved, leadership has rotated amongst several participants.

Step IV: After approximately three months, an assessment of the effectiveness of this process was made by asking all participants for feedback. The overwhelming response was positive. Participants felt that many problems were being prevented and resolved expediently, communication had improved significantly, and the development of positive relationships was occurring. In addition, other internal suppliers joined the huddle as the need for their involvement was identified. The flexibility of this methodology allows for the group to invite anyone throughout the organization to attend a huddle on an as-needed basis. Non-management personnel have become more involved as the process matured.

Step V: The Organizational Huddle™ expanded into several departmental units. This process is informal, and departments that truly embrace this methodology should drive expansion efforts. I recommend that you allow for and become comfortable with the natural evolution of this process.

Outcomes:

To date, over five hundred problems have been quickly resolved. The following are a few examples:

1) STAT medication orders expedited
2) Instituted hemoccult point-of-care testing

3) Par levels on omnicell units adjusted to ensure stock availability
4) Standardized nursing unit pharmacy drop-off of medications
5) Reorganized patient belonging storage area in security

Other Benefits Include:

- Development of strong interdisciplinary collaborative relationships
- Foster empowerment and accountability within the culture of the organization
- Increase in stakeholder satisfaction

Organization 3 – Health System in Pennsylvania

This organization was very interested in achieving the objectives of the Huddle. Their goals are to identify minor operational problems before they cause a major crisis hospital-wide, foster interdisciplinary collaboration across many departments, and resolve problems expeditiously.

The prior practice at this organization was to set up multiple Nursing interdisciplinary committees to meet the objective of solving small operational problems. Existing were the Nursing Lab committee and the Nursing-Radiology committee, to name a few. The committees started by meeting monthly, but as time passed, they became less and less frequent, and follow up on issues identified at earlier meetings were somehow lost.

I was contacted to assist in implementation of the huddle as a means of meeting desired goals, and the potential elimination of several interdisciplinary meetings.

Two nurse managers assumed the role of internal champions at their hospital with the full support of the vice president of Patient Care Services.

The decision was to create an interdisciplinary huddle comprised of Nursing and several support departments, scheduled to huddle three times per week at 8:45 AM in the cafeteria. Consistent with the huddle process, no agenda or meetings are used. Issues are tracked highlighting the departments involved, whether the concern was resolved or tabled, or presented to the Performance Improvement Team.

Outcomes:

To date, over four hundred issues have been quickly resolved. The following are a few examples:

1) IV Team: A representative brought new physician order sheets that are to be initiated in all patient care areas. This was a great way to disseminate information in a timely manner and assist in a getting the new project off to a smooth start.
2) The vice president of Support Services announced the upcoming parking lot renovations to improve availability for their customers. A review of hospital policy regarding Department of Health visits was also covered.
3) The Material Management representative resolved ongoing issues with the supply chain on nursing units. Issues addressed included par levels of patient care supplies, emergency supply availability, and procedure for handling off hour patient care supply needs.
4) Timeliness of cleaning of discharge beds was resolved. This has decreased the wait time of patients in the PACU and ER.

Other Benefits Include:

- Several previously existing interdisciplinary meetings have been eliminated.
- Development of strong interdisciplinary collaboration.
- Huddle expansion into another hospital site.

The following poem was submitted by this organization:

Along came the idea of a Huddle,
The process we were charged to start.
A meeting of management 'round a table
Many issues we do impart.

The issues are discussed as needed,
In hopes that they will be resolved.
Some concerns are tabled 'til next time,
Some are brought back by those involved.

The process has proven successful
In the short time we have met.
We hope that others can take from us
The guidelines we have set.

A big thanks goes to all our supporters,
And especially to our guide, Bob Cooper.
We enjoy our huddles to the max,
Plus our outcomes have been just super!

Organization 4 – Hospital in Connecticut

The Critical Care Division at this hospital identified an opportunity to achieve a higher level of sophistication as a health care team. They realized that they were in the midst of a challenging time in health care as a result of the increasing nursing shortage, patient acuity, and volume of patient throughput in and out of Critical Care. These challenges, coupled with an environment of decreasing health care reimbursement and an increasingly competitive marketplace, made them realize the need to develop new skills as a team.

Two days were set aside off campus for a Critical Care Retreat. During the retreat, members of the interdisciplinary team from the MSICU and Intermediate Care Units gathered to identify and learn the essential skills of a highly functioning team. The Huddle process was introduced as the primary methodology for teambuilding. Improving communications within the day-to-day operations of the unit was identified as a key objective. The makeup of the nursing staff was changing with the addition of temporary staff and new hire orientees to the team. Management was committed to improving team relationships and being more responsive and effective in their communication.

The principles of the Organizational Huddle™ are based on straight talk, honesty, respect and accountability to all members of the team. The Critical Care team decided that the Huddle process would assist in incorporating these principles into their daily work. The methodology of the Huddle was introduced and there was general enthusiasm, particularly from those who participated in the retreat.

Outcomes:

- *Staff satisfaction has been very positively impacted* in the Critical Care Division since the huddle has been implemented.
- Staff are empowered to "seize the moment" to resolve concerns and accountability, and teamwork has been enhanced.

The following are a few examples of issues resolved:

1) In Intermediate Care Unit, the RN's and NA's working relationship has improved. They identified that the source of their problems was miscommunication.
2) In the ICU, a surgeon required specific supplies and equipment that was not normally kept on the unit, thus delaying certain procedures. The huddle quickly created a surgeon-specific kit that is currently stocked in the pyxsis supply station, thereby eliminating the problem.

3) A planned discussion was implemented at the beginning of the shift to identify the staff member who will be attending that day's educational offering. It is also predetermined how the patient assignments of that staff member would be redistributed.

Organization 5 – Medical Center in New York

This organization initiated the Huddle process to expedite problem solving and teach management staff to become more accountable to each other. Departments had not always viewed each other as internal customers, thus creating conflict with many problems remaining unresolved.

The Human Resources Department decided to take the lead in initiating the Huddle methodology. An interdisciplinary huddle involving Human Resources with several key departments was formed. This has further enhanced Human Resources as a proactive business partner and has facilitated fast decision making to improve hospital operations.

Outcomes:

To date, over one hundred problems have been addressed. The following are a few examples:

1) Creation of a private room for doctors to consult with patients in the ICU
2) Monitor crash carts to avoid patient or staff injuries
3) In-service for staff regarding hospital directory
4) Expedite tray removal from several units

Final Thoughts

The time has come to turn the ball over to those closest to the customer, remove obstacles, and get out of the way. The best coaches know that games are ultimately won or lost based on the contributions of the players on the field. I believe it is the responsibility of leaders to provide employees with the opportunity to step onto the playing field. When we collaborate effectively and build relationships, we all become champions. The costs are minimal and the results are phenomenal. This simply makes good business sense. Your employees and customers all want to enjoy the feeling of being at and winning the Superbowl, you can show them the way!

Frequently Asked Questions

Q: What is the difference between a huddle and a meeting?
A: The huddle is an ongoing process that does not have an agenda and no minutes are taken. The huddle has a start time and is not to exceed thirty minutes (although the huddle usually ends in ten to fifteen minutes). The huddle is focused on internal customer relationships with everyone serving as an equal participant regardless of formal title.

Q: How do you select the leader?
A: Leadership should be rotated or at the very least assumed over time by several participants. In the initial start-up phase, the champion(s) will assume leadership for the first few huddles. It is important to advise participants that leadership is to be shared and show that this is not an onerous task. As a huddle matures, participants do not have to predetermine leadership until they arrive at the session. Anyone can ask, "Who is going to lead?" You will find that several individuals do not mind and even enjoy the leader role.

Q: What do we do if no problems are raised?
A: Remind participants that this is an ongoing process. Acknowledging that no new problems have arisen is a

positive indication that customers' needs are being met. Also use this as another opportunity to remind individuals that the face to face communication created through this process builds relationships. Even when no new issues emerge, you will find that someone usually will provide an update or thank someone for their assistance. Some huddles are quite dynamic, with many issues raised and a feeling of great accomplishment, while others will be very fast with few tangible issues resolved. In either case, it is important for participants to see both as a success.

Q: How do I get started?
A: The first step is to hold an information session with senior management to discuss the goals and objectives of this methodology. Include in this meeting suggestions of potential pilot huddle(s) and why you believe this would be in the best interest for the organization. It is essential to attain management full support prior to commencing the process. Champions need to be selected and trained on all aspects of the Huddle methodology. The champions serve as a liaison between senior management and the huddle, with responsibility for oversight of the process. The next step is to meet with the pilot huddle(s) and their respective managers to review the process. They will need to receive comprehensive training on the Huddle process. Attain agreement on which departments or job classifications will be represented at the huddle, and determine huddle times and location. Hold the first huddle session, using this as an opportunity for participants to begin getting comfortable with the process. At this point you are off and running. It is vital that participants stay with the process and are reminded that it will take time for all to become fully comfortable. The speed at which the process will take hold is dependent to a large extent on the organization's existing culture. If collaboration through mutual trust, respect, and accountability is prevalent throughout the organization, the Huddle will most likely go smoothly from the very beginning. On the other hand, if the culture is not

founded on the aforementioned principles, this methodology can and will serve to move the culture in that direction as long as full management support is in place for the individual(s) responsible for implementation.

Testimonials

"The strength of the Huddle concept in healthcare is that it plays to tactics-making decisions on the field in real time. Like the world of sports, the ability to lead under fire far surpasses strategy sessions spent around calm table dialogue. I have found that the Huddle identifies problems, facilitates operational decisions, and builds trust."

> Richard Birrer, M.D., President and CEO
> St. Joseph's Health Care System

"When Bob first introduced the Huddle to our organization, we were facing new competition for multi-functional products. Interfunctional communication was an essential element to our success. Bob coached the team on the concepts of the Huddle. This has made our people think more as a team, act more quickly, and with much less meeting 'downtime.'"

> Marc Mackin, Executive Vice President
> Lapp USA, Inc.

"We made a commitment at all levels to adopt the fundamental principles of effective communication of the Huddle process:

honesty, respect and accountability. This has absolutely enhanced our effectiveness as a team as we can communicate more directly and respond more rapidly."

> Peggy Martino, Program Director, Cardiology/Medicine
> Greenwich Hospital

"The Critical Care staff has completed training of the Huddle technique. It is my impression that this is a useful technique in dealing with issues on the units in a quick, direct and straightforward manner. It facilitates patient care."

> Quinton Friesen, Sr., Vice President/Chief Operating Officer
> Greenwich Hospital

"The beauty of the Huddle is it provides an opportunity for excellent interaction at a retreat setting with carry-through back at the workplace. The two together allow for a process of positive change to occur."

> Steven Shelov, M.D., Chairman, Department of Pediatrics
> Maimonides Medical Center

"We have accomplished so much since we started the Huddle process, and we were able to cut out multiple meetings from our busy schedules."

> Theresa Sellers, Nurse Manager, Telemetry Unit
> Community General Osteopathic Hospital

"We have solved many problems in the last eight months and have developed a better working relationship with other department managers."

> Kim Orfanelli, Nurse Manager, Orthopedics Unit
> Community General Osteopathic Hospital

"The Huddle has created a great sense of accountability for fast problem resolution, increased employee morale and excitement with the process, and an appreciation for the challenges others face within the organization."

    Marchene Noel, Director, Human Resources
    Interfaith Medical Center

RL Cooper Associates offers comprehensive training and consultative support to ensure effective implementation of the Organizational Huddle™. Please contact RL Cooper Associates at:

    RL Cooper Associates
    (845) 639-1741
    info@rlcooperassoc.com
    www.rlcooperassoc.com